# REALISTIC ROCK FOR KIDS

This book is lovingly dedicated to my kids, **Nicholas** and **Bianca**, and all the kids and future drummers of the world!

Exclusively Distributed by Alfred Music Publishing Co., Inc.
Printed in USA.

Alfred Music
P.O. Box 10003
Van Nuys, CA 91410-0003
alfred.com

ISBN-10: 0-7579-9460-1
ISBN-13: 978-0-7579-9460-9

# CARMINE ENDORSES:

| | |
|---|---|
| ddrum Signature Products | Rhythm Tech Products |
| Vic Firth Signature Sticks | Dean Guitar Products |
| Sabian Signature Cymbals | Calzone Cases |
| Evans Drumheads | Zoom/Samson Products |
| Shure Mics | Protechtor Cases |
| DW Pedals | Big Bang Products |

# CARMINE WOULD LIKE TO THANK:

Link Harnsberger, Ron Manus, John O'Reilly Jr., Rich Lackowski, Michael Finkelstein, and Bryan Bradley at Alfred Music Publishing; David Hakim; Ray Brych; Leslie, Bianca, and Nicholas; all my endorsement companies; and all the rockin' kids who use this book!

Edited by - RICK GRATTON

Book Layout & Music Engraving - RICK GRATTON

Artwork - THE GRAPHIC MILL & RICK GRATTON

Carmine Illustrations - BILL PHILIPOVICH

Audio Recording and Mixing - SOUND ASYLUM

Engineer - STEVE (THE LUNATIC) WERBELOW

CDs Produced by - CARMINE APPICE

## PLAY-ALONG MUSICIANS:

Bass - TONY FRANKLIN

Guitar - STEVE FISTER

For more information please visit: www.carmineappice.net

# IN THIS BOOK

# GRADUATION CERTIFICATE!

Hi, my name is **Carmine Appice**, and welcome to

# REALISTIC ROCK FOR KIDS.

Starting today, I will teach you how to play drums! Soon you'll be playing along with your favorite songs or your own band! This book shows you how to play rock 'n' roll drums the **quick and easy way!** I've included two practice CDs to help you understand and apply the lessons.

So, the sooner we start, the sooner you'll learn.

## LET'S ROCK!

# THE BASICS

Here are the note and rest values
used in this book:

Quarter notes = one beat = quarter-note rest
Eighth notes = half of a beat = eighth-note rest

**COUNTING:** We use numbers when we count each note.
The quarter notes have a different count from the eighth notes.
Count each quarter note with each number: 1, 2, 3, 4.
With the eighth-note count, you will notice an "&" between each number:
1 & 2 & 3 & 4 &. On CD 1, I will play an example of quarter and eighth notes
and will count them for you.

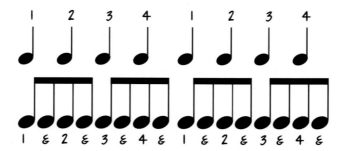

**RESTS:** When you see a rest, it means you should "say it" and not "play it."
**Example:** If we want to rest on number 2 and play numbers 1, 3, 4, it would look like this:
1 REST 3 4. As you can see, you leave out beat 2 and tap beats 1, 3, 4.
**A MEASURE or BAR:** A measure is a total of four beats counted 1, 2, 3, 4.
**MUSIC LINES:** For most of the book, there are three lines
that show us what drums we are going to play.

**LINE 0** is the TOM-TOM.

**LINE 1** is the HI-HAT (HH).

**LINE 2** is the SNARE DRUM (SD).

**LINE 3** is the BASS DRUM (BD).

Here is what they look like:

| | |
|---|---|
| TOM LINE 0 | |
| HH LINE 1 | |
| SD LINE 2 | |
| BD LINE 3 | |

# REPEAT MARKS

We use two repeat marks throughout the book:

1. Repeat the bar or measure before:

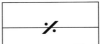

2. Repeat the bar or measure itself:

 When you see this face logo, it tells you which TRACK NUMBER to follow along with on the CDs!

# HOLDING THE DRUMSTICKS

To hold the sticks, first pick them up with both hands, one in each hand with your palms facing down. Make sure you don't squeeze the sticks too tightly, just enough to wrap your fingers around them as if you were holding on to them like a pair of handlebars on a bicycle. It's that easy! Check out the drawing below.

## A BASIC DRUM SET

THE DRUM SET

## THE KEY TO DRUMMING

DRUM KEY

This drawing shows you which drum to play on each line in a bar or measure.

# SECTION 1

## QUARTER-NOTE GROOVES

# QUARTER NOTES

## QUARTER-NOTE GROOVES

Listen to the CD to hear how to play the beat below.
**The quarter notes are counted 1, 2, 3, 4.**
**The eighth notes are counted 1 & 2 & 3 & 4 &.**
The beats between the hands and feet are quarter notes, counted 1, 2, 3, 4.

Watch for the rest, where you **don't** play. I have written out four exercises. Each exercise has eight bars of music including two repeat bars. Have fun playing these patterns over and over.

### LET'S GET STARTED!

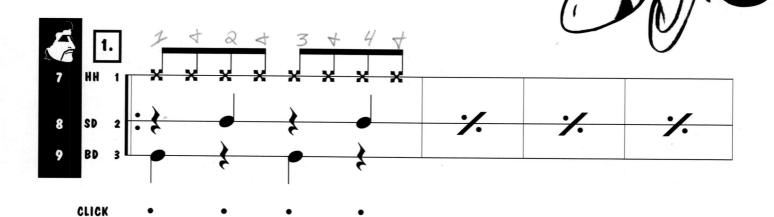

**NOW YOU...**

1  2  3  4

**TRACK 10: COMPLETE EX. 1 ALL TOGETHER**

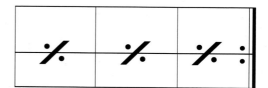

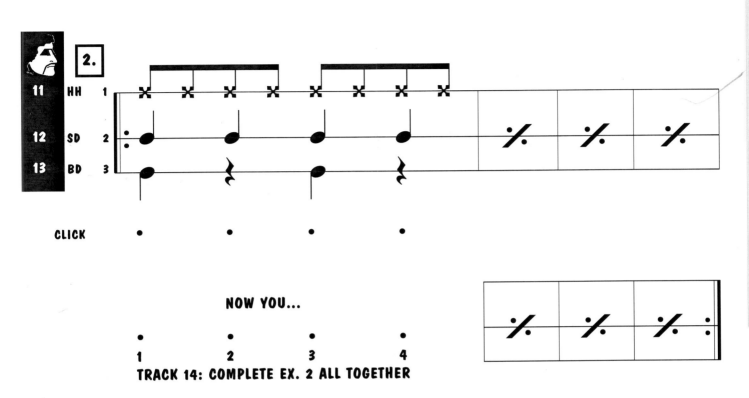

**2.**

11 HH 1
12 SD 2
13 BD 3

CLICK

NOW YOU...

1    2    3    4

TRACK 14: COMPLETE EX. 2 ALL TOGETHER

QUARTER NOTES

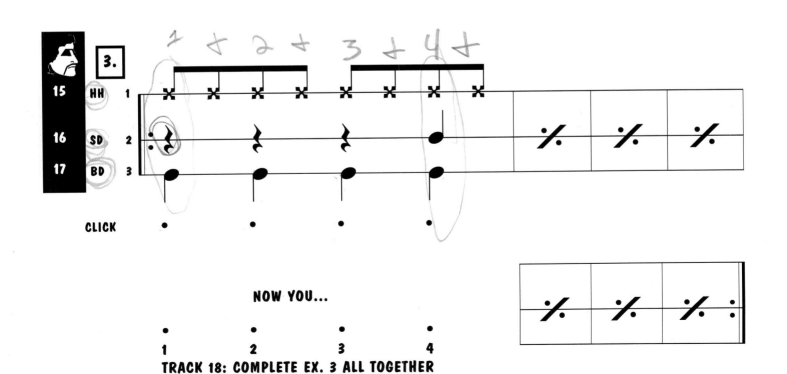

**3.**

15 HH 1
16 SD 2
17 BD 3

CLICK

NOW YOU...

1    2    3    4

TRACK 18: COMPLETE EX. 3 ALL TOGETHER

# QUARTER-NOTE GROOVES

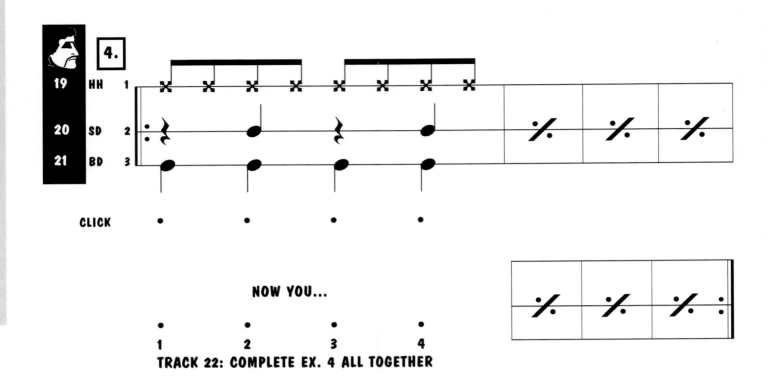

NOW YOU...

1     2     3     4

**TRACK 22: COMPLETE EX. 4 ALL TOGETHER**

# SECTION 2

# EIGHTH-NOTE GROOVES

# EIGHTH-NOTE GROOVES

**EIGHTH NOTES**

## EIGHTH-NOTE GROOVES

Next we will play eighth notes between our hands and feet. These notes are counted **1 & 2 & 3 & 4 &.** Listen to the CD for help. I've written out nine exercises with two repeat marks for each pattern. Play each beat over and over, and pay attention to the eighth-note rests.

**One more thing:** On the CD there is a click to help you with the tempo. I'll play along with you. After I play for four bars with the click, the click will keep playing, and that's where you play along with it. I will be counting along with each exercise.

### HERE WE GO!

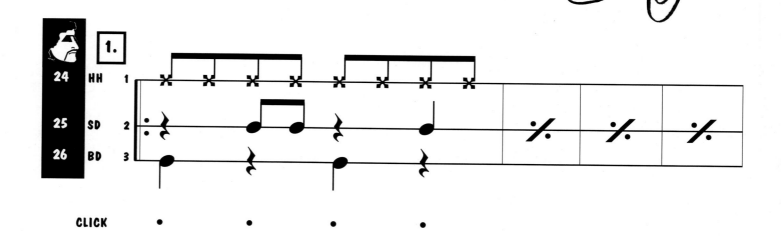

CLICK

**NOW YOU...**

1    2    3    4

**TRACK 27: COMPLETE EX. 1 ALL TOGETHER**

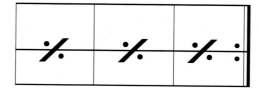

**2.**

28 HH 1
29 SD 2
30 BD 3

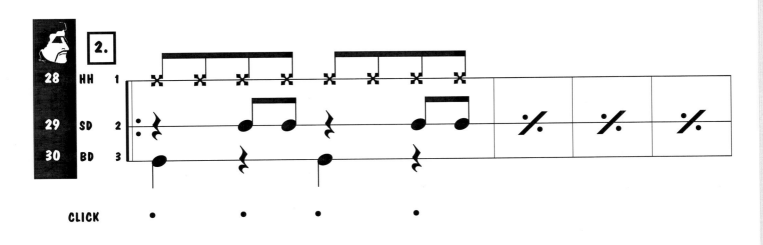

CLICK

NOW YOU...

1    2    3    4

TRACK 31: COMPLETE EX. 2 ALL TOGETHER

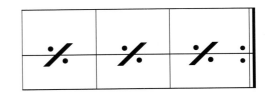

**EIGHTH NOTES**

**3.**

32 HH 1
33 SD 2
34 BD 3

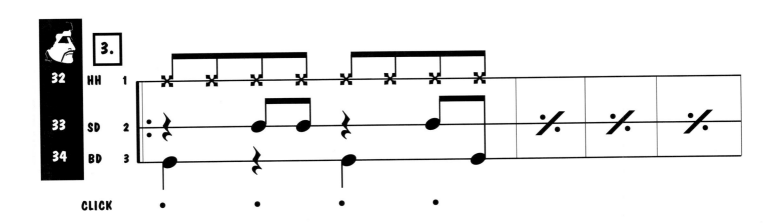

CLICK

NOW YOU...

1    2    3    4

TRACK 35: COMPLETE EX. 3 ALL TOGETHER

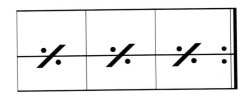

# EIGHTH-NOTE GROOVES

EIGHTH NOTES

**4.**

36 HH 1

SD 2

37 BD 3

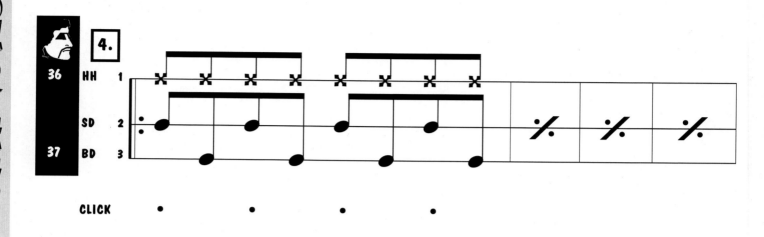

CLICK

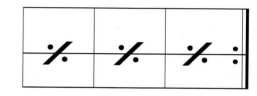

NOW YOU...

1    2    3    4

**TRACK 38: COMPLETE EX. 4 ALL TOGETHER**

**5.**

39 HH 1

SD 2

40 BD 3

CLICK

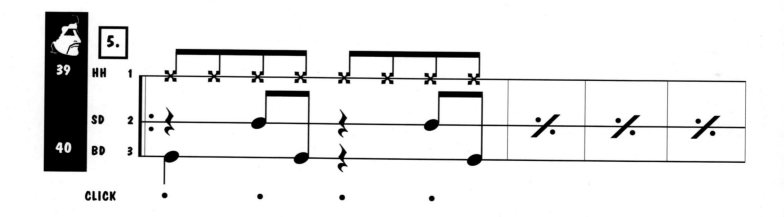

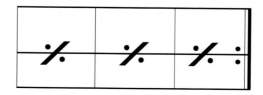

NOW YOU...

1    2    3    4

**TRACK 41: COMPLETE EX. 5 ALL TOGETHER**

**6.**

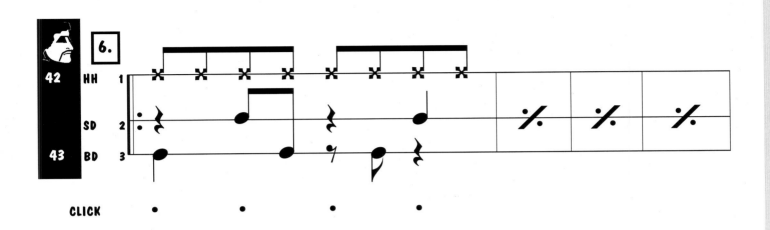

NOW YOU...

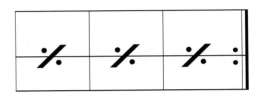

1    2    3    4

**TRACK 44: COMPLETE EX. 6 ALL TOGETHER**

**7.**

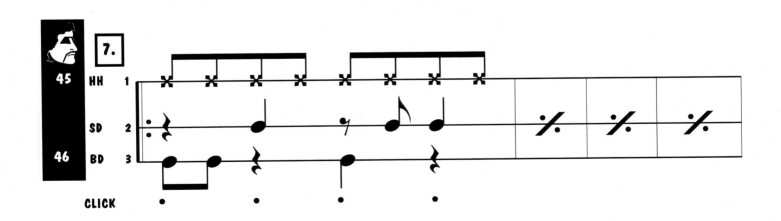

NOW YOU...

1    2    3    4

**TRACK 47: COMPLETE EX. 7 ALL TOGETHER**

# EIGHTH-NOTE GROOVES

**EIGHTH NOTES**

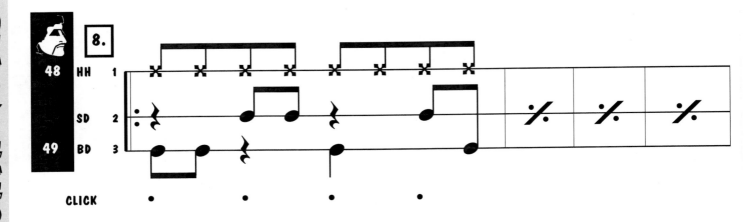

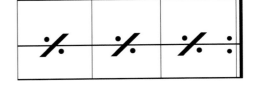

NOW YOU...

• • • •
1    2    3    4
**TRACK 50: COMPLETE EX. 8 ALL TOGETHER**

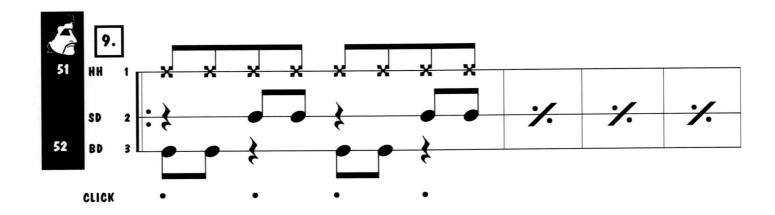

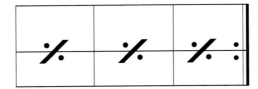

NOW YOU...

• • • •
1    2    3    4
**TRACK 53: COMPLETE EX. 9 ALL TOGETHER**

# BONUS EXERCISES
# TWO-BAR PATTERNS

TWO-BAR PATTERNS

The double repeat sign means to REPEAT the first two bars here!

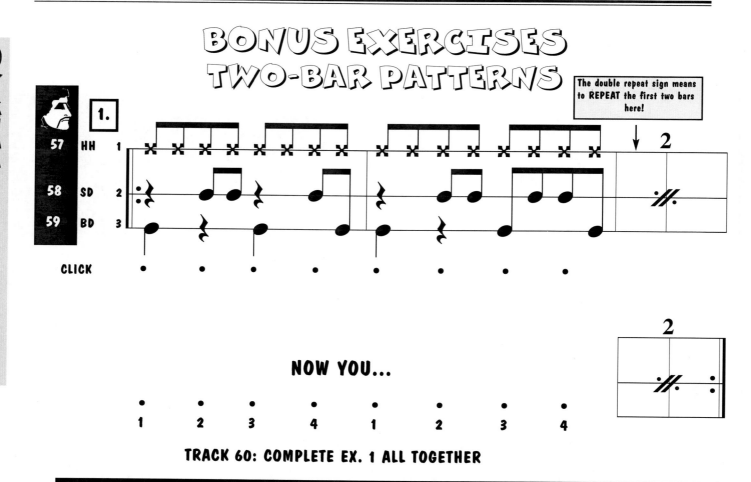

**NOW YOU...**

1    2    3    4    1    2    3    4

TRACK 60: COMPLETE EX. 1 ALL TOGETHER

**NOW YOU...**

1    2    3    4    1    2    3    4

TRACK 63: COMPLETE EX. 2 ALL TOGETHER

# SECTION 3

## MY FIRST DRUM FILLS
## MY FIRST DRUM SOLO

# MY FIRST DRUM FILLS

# MY FIRST DRUM FILLS

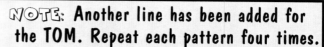

**NOTE:** Another line has been added for the TOM. Repeat each pattern four times.

**NOW YOU...**

**NOW YOU...**

# MY FIRST DRUM FILLS

DRUM FILLS

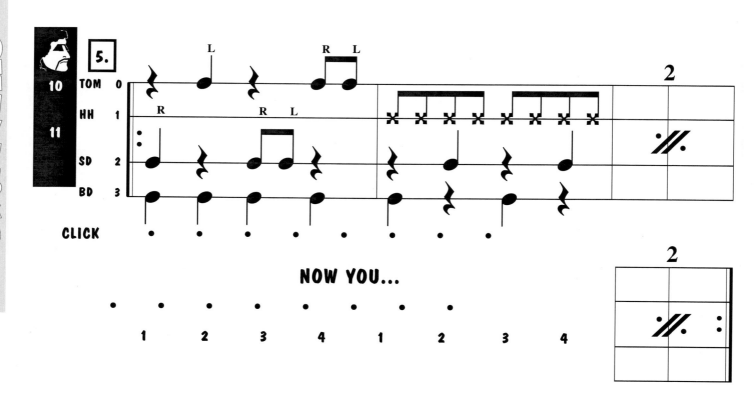

NOW YOU...

25

# MY FIRST DRUM SOLO

Play the groove on the CD and play the solo on the next page. The song or groove has a click, a bass, and a guitar on it. You can follow along with the song on the CD, and here is how to do it: Play eight bars of any groove that you like, and then play the 16-bar solo (written out for you on the next page), then eight bars of groove, and then it ends.

Listening to the CD over and over will be a great help. Say out loud, "BOOM BOOM BOP BOP, BOOM BOOM BOP BOP," and this will help you get a good feeling for the solo. Please listen to CD 2, Track 12, and then

# LET'S GO SOLO

# MY FIRST DRUM SOLO

12

13 - WITH DRUMS - SLOW

14 - NOW YOU - SLOW

15 - NOW YOU - FAST

Pick a groove and play it eight times along with the CD
and then play the SOLO below!

# SOLO

DRUM SOLO

**BACK TO GROOVE FOR EIGHT BARS**

**PLAY-ALONG SONGS:**

**16** - GROOVE SONG-GROOVE #1 - SLOW

**17** - GROOVE SONG-GROOVE #1 - FAST

**18** - GROOVE WILD SIDE #2 - SLOW

**19** - GROOVE WILD SIDE #2 - FAST

**20** - GROOVE GROOVE - SLOW

**21** - GROOVE GROOVE - FAST

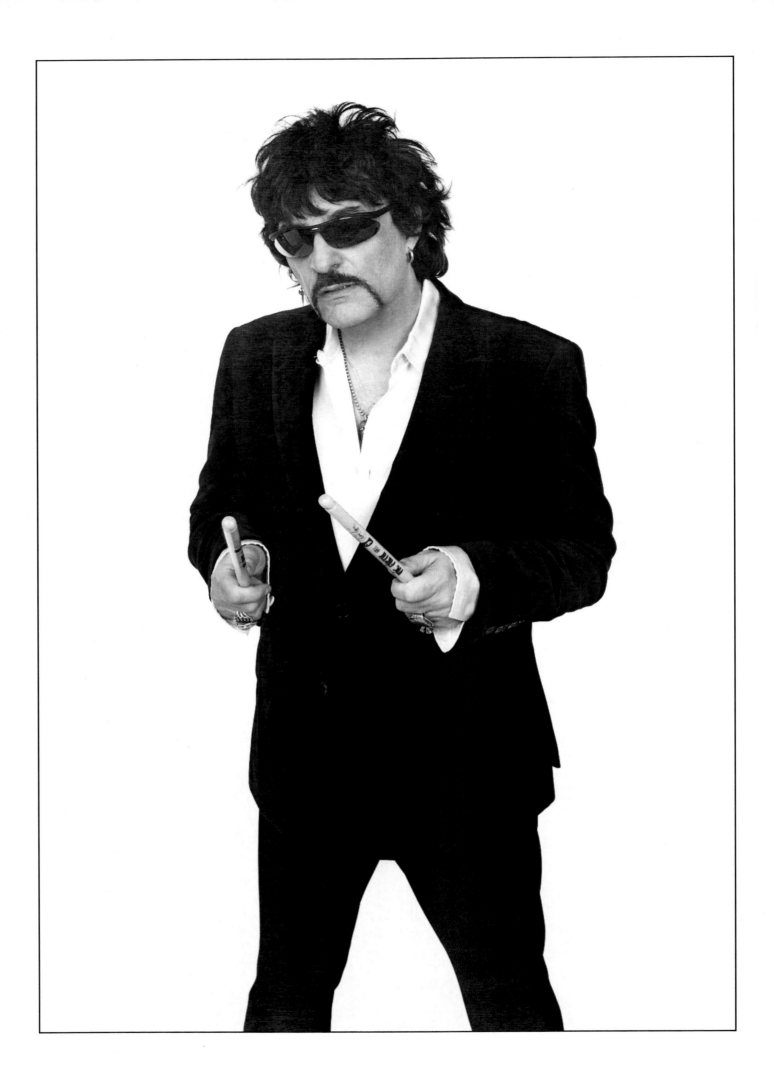

# CD SEQUENCE INSTRUCTION

## CD 1

### TRACK # SECTION 1

| | |
|---|---|
| 1 | Welcome |
| 2 | The basics - note values |
| 3 | Definitions, rests, measures, tempo, click |
| 4 | Holding the sticks |
| 5 | The drum set and play-along songs |
| 6 | Quarter notes |
| 7 | Ex 1   hi-hat |
| 8 | Ex 1   snare drum |
| 9 | Ex 1   bass drum |
| 10 | Ex 1   complete |
| 11 | Ex 2   hi-hat |
| 12 | Ex 2   snare drum |
| 13 | Ex 2   bass drum |
| 14 | Ex 2   complete |
| 15 | Ex 3   hi-hat |
| 16 | Ex 3   snare drum |
| 17 | Ex 3   bass drum |
| 18 | Ex 3   complete |
| 19 | Ex 4   hi-hat |
| 20 | Ex 4   snare drum |
| 21 | Ex 4   bass drum |
| 22 | Ex 4   complete |

## CD 1

### TRACK # SECTION 2

| | |
|---|---|
| 23 | Eighth notes |
| 24 | Ex 1   hi-hat |
| 25 | Ex 1   snare drum |
| 26 | Ex 1   bass drum |
| 27 | Ex 1   complete |
| 28 | Ex 2   hi-hat |
| 29 | Ex 2   snare drum |
| 30 | Ex 2   bass drum |
| 31 | Ex 2   complete |
| 32 | Ex 3   hi-hat |
| 33 | Ex 3   snare drum |
| 34 | Ex 3   bass drum |
| 35 | Ex 3   complete |
| 36 | Ex 4   hi-hat |
| | Ex 4   snare drum |
| 37 | Ex 4   bass drum |
| 38 | Ex 4   complete |
| 39 | Ex 5   hi-hat |
| | Ex 5   snare drum |
| 40 | Ex 5   bass drum |
| 41 | Ex 5   complete |
| 42 | Ex 6   hi-hat |
| | Ex 6   snare drum |
| 43 | Ex 6   bass drum |
| 44 | Ex 6   complete |
| 45 | Ex 7   hi-hat |
| | Ex 7   snare drum |
| 46 | Ex 7   bass drum |
| 47 | Ex 7   complete |
| 48 | Ex 8   hi-hat |
| | Ex 8   snare drum |
| 49 | Ex 8   bass drum |
| 50 | Ex 8   complete |
| 51 | Ex 9   hi-hat |
| | Ex 9   snare drum |
| 52 | Ex 9   bass drum |
| 53 | Ex 9   complete |
| 54 | Review exercise talk |
| 55 | Exercises 1–16, bar Ex |
| 56 | Now you play |
| 57 | Bonus exercise talk |
| 58 | Ex 1   hi-hat |
| | Ex 1   snare drum |
| 59 | Ex 1   bass drum |
| 60 | Ex 1   complete |
| 61 | Ex 2   hi-hat |
| | Ex 2   snare drum |
| 62 | Ex 2   bass drum |
| 63 | Ex 2   complete |

**END CD 1**

## CD 2

### TRACK # SECTION 3

| | |
|---|---|
| 1 | My first drum fill intro |
| 2 | Ex 1   demo info |
| 3 | Ex 1   fill & time |
| 4 | Ex 2   demo |
| 5 | Ex 2   fill & time |
| 6 | Ex 3   add tom |
| | Ex 3   demo |
| 7 | Ex 3   fill & time |
| 8 | Ex 4   demo |
| 9 | Ex 4   fill & time |
| 10 | Ex 5   demo talk |
| 11 | Ex 5   fill & time |
| 12 | My first drum solo - demo |
| 13 | My first drum solo - demo |
| 14 | Now you - slow |
| 15 | Now you - fast |

### PLAY-ALONG SONGS

| | |
|---|---|
| 16 | Groove Song |
| | Groove #1 - Slow |
| 17 | Groove Song |
| | Groove #1 - Fast |
| 18 | Groove Wild |
| | Side #2 - Slow |
| 19 | Groove Wild |
| | Side #2 - Fast |
| 20 | Groove |
| | Groove - Slow |
| 21 | Groove |
| | Groove - Fast |

**END CD 2**

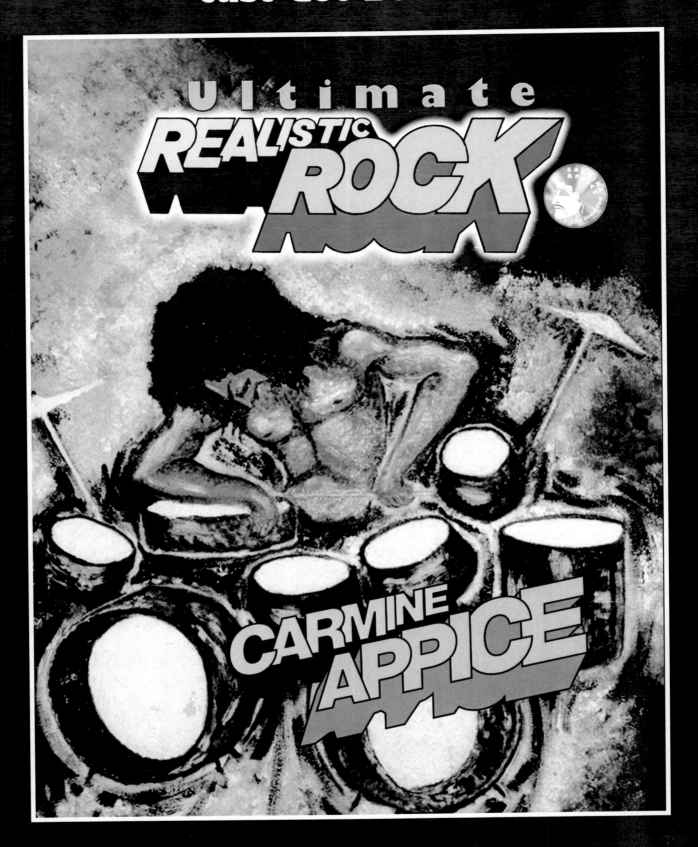

# Certificate of Achievement

This certifies that

_____

has successfully completed

**REALISTIC ROCK FOR KIDS**

You can now graduate to

**ULTIMATE REALISTIC ROCK**

_Carmine Appice_

Carmine Appice